VENTURING DUCKS

The book about a book.
You too can follow your dreams you just have to believe you can!

Copyright © 2024 by Venturing Ducks

All rights reserved. No part of this publication may be reproduced, stored or transmitted in any form or by any means, electronic, mechanical, photocopying, recording, scanning, or otherwise without written permission from the publisher. It is illegal to copy this book, post it to a website, or distribute it by any other means without permission.

Photo on the front cover was taken by the author at Eungella Dam, Queensland.

First edition

This book was professionally typeset on Reedsy. Find out more at reedsy.com

A dream can be dreamed,
An arrow can be followed,
Any path can be chosen,
Your life can be what you want it to be.
All you have to do is believe.
A.H.

For all those who believed in me.

For all those needing inspiration to believe in themselves.

Contents

Introduction	1
Part 1 B.C.	2
South Australia	4
Northern Territory	6
Victoria	8
Tasmania	10
Queensland	13
Queensland still	15
Victoria again	17
Back to Queensland	19
Western Australia	21
Western Australia still - but just up the road	23
Victoria and Queensland	25
Queensland- Back to Moranbah	27
Part 2 A.C.	30
Lucky9	32
CatDuck	34
Mackay - Queensland	36
Plans change	40
The new plan	44
Kindle Direct Publishing- KDP	45
Amazon	48
The book about a book	50
The End	52

Introduction

The book about a book
You too can follow your dreams you just have to believe you can!

If you are looking for a formal, professional book with all the fancy editing, this isn't it.

It's just me an Aussie woman writing my book, my way.

However, if you are looking for inspiration and a don't give up story, then by all means, turn the page! Its only a short story, but it might just be the answer to a lifelong dream.

Yes, this book is about a book, but more than that, it is about dreams and your choice to follow them or give up and then wonder what if.

Part 1 B.C.

Before Covid-
Don't worry, this book is not about Covid, it just makes a good timeline marker for the 2 parts of the book.

A bit like the fairy tales of old this story has a "Once upon a time" start to it, why you ask? It's not a fairytale!

Well, I feel like it's important to understand how I got to where I am now, why I want to get where I am going, and how this book will help me.

Part 1 B.C.

This is my map of Australia, it is also a record of my life, and a dream to fulfill.

South Australia

My Mum and Dad were working on a cattle station in South Australia when I was born at a little country town called Bordertown.

I have never seen this town, but it is on my list to visit. Obviously, I don't remember anything from the station, but the story goes that I spent a lot of time in the chook yard in my pram, or out watching the calves in the paddock.

No Netflix back then! And I cried A LOT!

South Australia

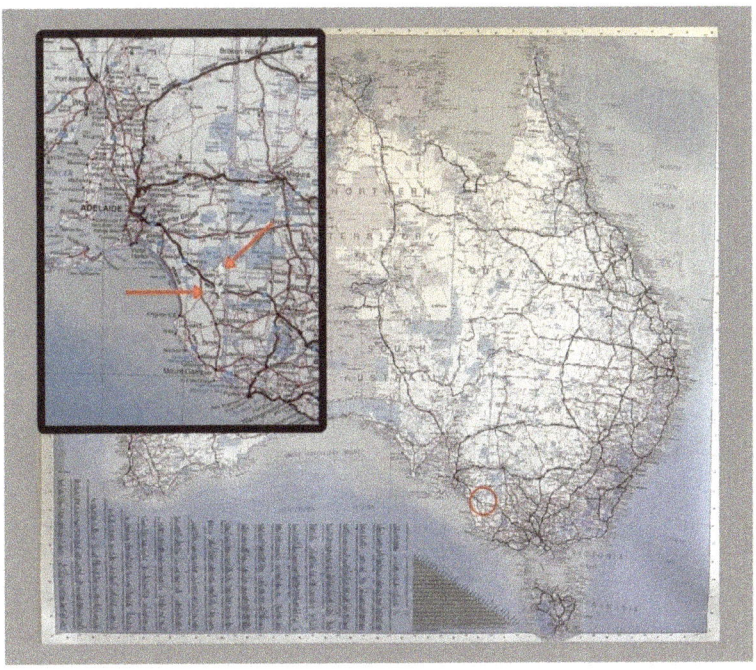

Northern Territory

Around 8 months old we moved up to Alice Springs in the Northern Territory and I had my first birthday living in a caravan, before my folks bought a house. They had some good friends up there and we did a lot of camping. Just swags in the bush. But I'm sure I would have loved it.

Northern Territory

Victoria

A couple of years later we moved south to a 40-acre farm at Avoca in Victoria. No electricity here, a generator and bore water, reading by candle light at night and the chance to watch "A wonderful world of Disney" on a Sunday night as long as I had washed my hair!

I loved the farm. I was too young to remember most of it, but I know we bred Squabs in a tram, same as those ones from Melbourne. My first pushbike was made from parts my dad found at the dump, plus a brand-new set of pedals, those sharp ones that would come back round and get you with the spikes! It was so cool. I attended kindy, prep and grade 1 at the local primary school in Avoca.

Victoria

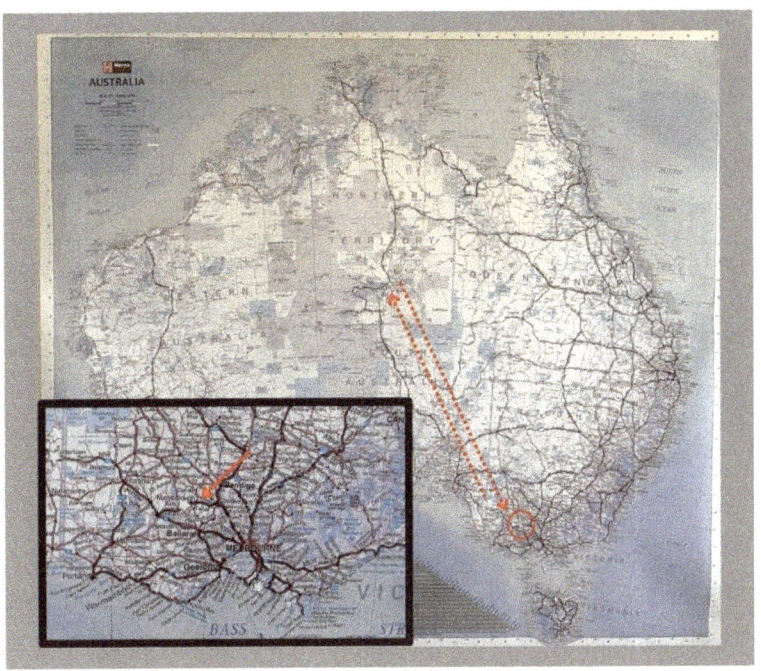

Tasmania

I think I was about 7 when we left there and moved to Port Sorell in Tasmania. Very different to the farm! We lived by the coast in a town. Dad had a yacht, and we would go away in that sometimes.

But my favorite thing to do was go on camping / fishing trips up to the Great Lakes with my dad. We would leave very early in the Land Rover, eating half of the marshmallows along the way, only the pink ones though, cause the white ones were to roast on the fire. We would arrive and set up camp, a couple of swags, a campfire and the fishing rods. That was it. So many tales from up there, like the one where the Bunyip jumped on me while I was sleeping in my swag one night, and the time I tried to reel in that BIG fish, that turned out to be a BIG sheet of ice! On the way back we would stop at the creeks and catch lobsters with meat tied to string, you needed a lot of patience for that, but it was worth the reward.

Sometimes in the school holidays I would fly on the little plane over to the mainland and stay with my Grandparents and

Tasmania

Aunty at Phillip Island while Mum and Dad still worked.

In Tassie I attended 3 different schools in 5 years, trying to find the one right for me.

In 1988 the conversation I remember was something about "do we go on a holiday or buy new carpet for the house." Still to this day I'm not 100% sure this conversation actually happened. But the decision was made for a holiday! And if I had been involved in it, that's what I would have chosen for sure.

Around my 11th birthday we made the trip from Tasmania to Queensland for Expo 88. My Uncle was living in Brisbane, and he showed us around the bottom half of the state.

Pretty sure I had the best journal from that trip, we explored so many places, I'm glad we never bought carpet. Why! Because not long after we got home a For Sale sign went up and yep, you guessed it, off we go to Qld.

Queensland

My Dad and I drove the truck up and we had this block of land at Rodds Harbour, you know one of those "it's the next big development" type places, but for now there was around 9 Adults and I think 1 kid me!

Dad and I lived in a caravan while we built a huge shed that we could live in, and I did Distance Education with a School of the Air.

Mum came up once she finished at her job in Tassie. She did not appreciate the cane toads that would hang around at dinner time.

Here I learnt to ride a little Honda motorbike and spent a lot of time catching yabbies with meat tied to string in the creek. Tiny compared to the lobsters but still an achievement when you caught them.

The book about a book.

Queensland still

That development didn't happen, work ran out so off we go again, staying in Qld but heading north-west to a mining town called Moranbah.

Mum and Dad had work on a cattle station that was outskirts of town and on the edge of a mine. I went to the local school in town, and when at home I could ride the little Honda out and meet Dad at the dams or wherever he was out fixing things.

Dad was doing maintenance and Mum would cook for the ringers. The year of my 13th birthday I graduated primary school. This was around the same time that something went down with my folks and they went separate ways.

The book about a book.

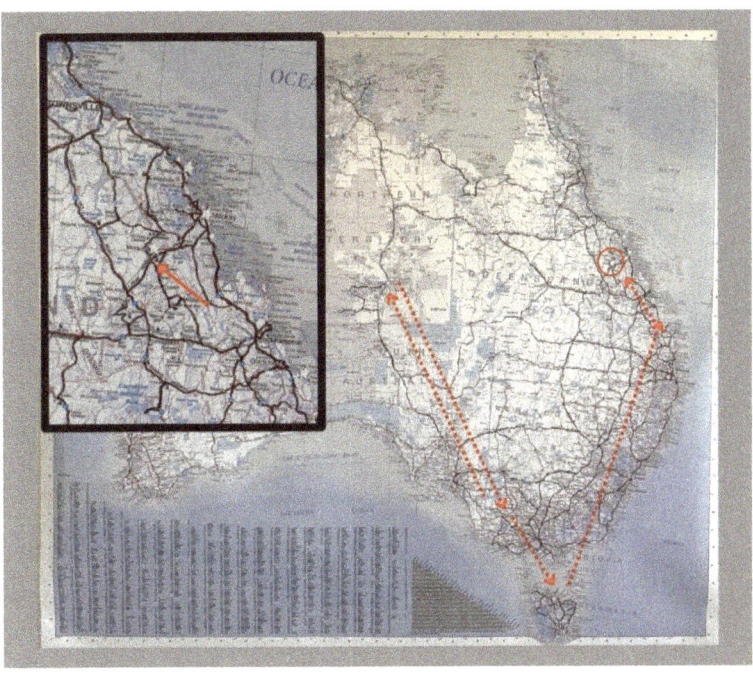

Victoria again

Mum headed to Airlie Beach. Dad and I drove down to Phillip Island, in Victoria, where a lot of his family were. I moved into a tiny caravan out the back on my Grandad's house and then at some point upgraded to a big one on the block next door, and then another van later that was out the back of the house my dad bought.

I started high school in Wonthaggi and stayed at the same school until I finished year 12. My constant reply for the question of "how was school?" was that "School is school" I wasn't pulling top marks, but I wasn't failing. I did work experience at a few places, but I was never sure what I wanted to do as a job. All I ever really wanted to do was travel.

At 14 I started waitressing at a restaurant where some of my family worked and it was there that I met my BFF of 32 years, at time of printing this book.

I loved hospitality and realised this could be my key to travel.

Year 12 finished, and I was out of there, 5 years in the one area, I had itchy feet.

The book about a book.

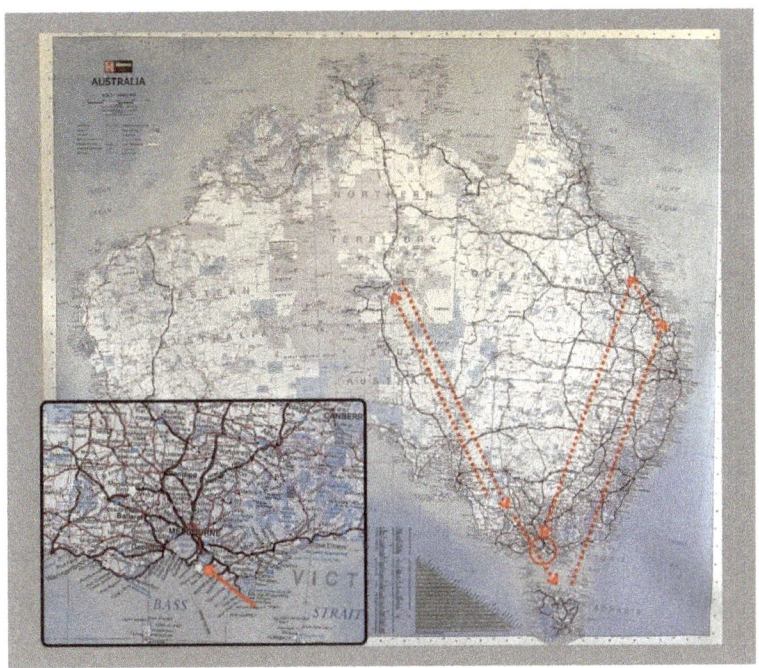

Back to Queensland

First stop, back up to Airlie Beach in Queensland where my mum was. This I soon realised was not going to work for me, 18 years old and a town of mainly bars and nightclubs and back then there was no such thing as a lock out times.

My days became a blur of working at a kebab shop, studying a certificate in hospitality, drinking, sleeping and repeating. Realising this wasn't how I wanted my life to go, off I headed again.

The book about a book.

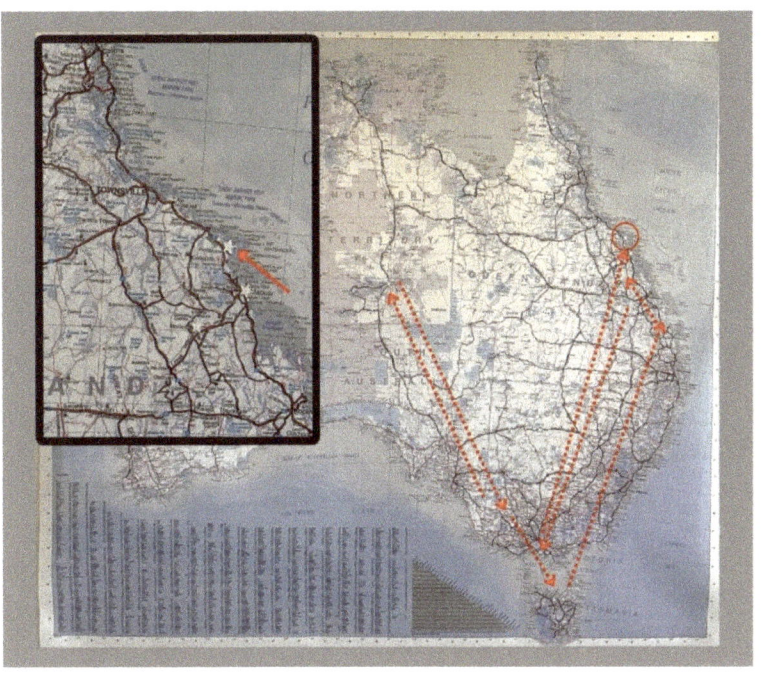

Western Australia

Where now? Western Australia, my BFF was now living here so it was an easy move to make. I started working at a motel chain in Mandurah, while I explored Perth and Rockingham. One of my favourite memories over here was watching a performance of 'A midsummer nights dream' in the Kings Park gardens in Perth. After a while I got offered a position at another motel further north in the same chain. Turns out it was a lot further north and a little west!

The book about a book.

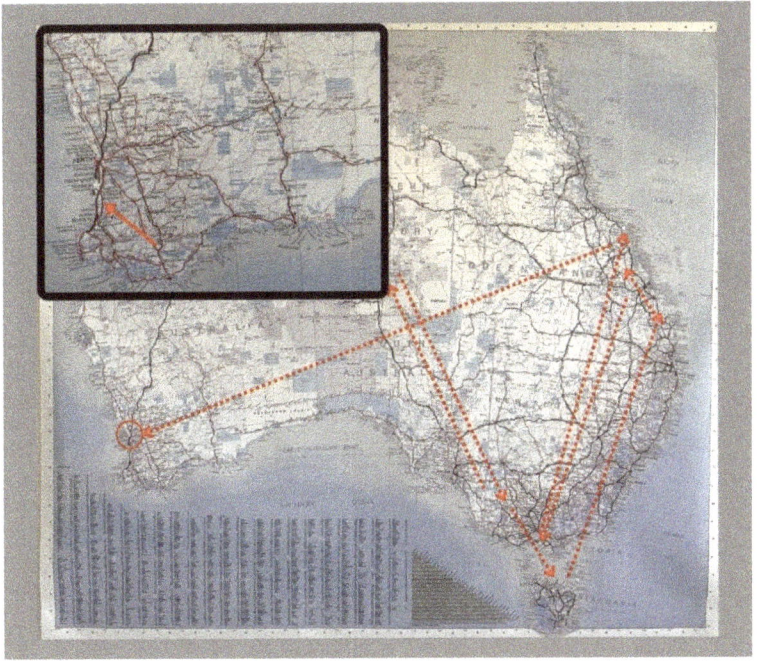

Western Australia still – but just up the road

Note to self, look up where the town is located before you say yes!

So now I am in Mt Newman which reminded me a lot of Moranbah. Only they had grass on their golf course, there was no grass in Newman!

While I was there I got a chance to go visit some of the spectacular gorges and Port Hedland. I was desperate to work at El Questro, but wasn't able to land a job there, i should have tried harder, I do regret giving up, but being quite young I was a little homesick for the east coast and so it was time to go.

The book about a book.

Victoria and Queensland

I headed back to Phillip Island and then Airlie Beach whilst trying to decide what to do with my life!

The book about a book.

Queensland– Back to Moranbah

The answer came with a call from an old school friend from Moranbah, who tells me a brand-new motel is getting built out there and they are looking for staff. Thinking this would look great on my resume I continue to contact the owner until he gives me a job as the Restaurant Manager.

You want something bad enough! Then don't just give up! Still to this day he tells the story of giving this young lady a chance to work for him because she continued to hound him for the job.

My plan. Work at the motel in Moranbah for 2 years, get a great reference then apply for the cruise ships and tour the world!

This all sounded like a great idea to me. I would get to travel work and see the world.

What I didn't plan for was the boy, that became the husband and then the father to our two amazing boys. Life had taken a turn down a different path.

However the traveling was still very prominent in my life.

The book about a book.

Lots of camping with friends and family. Road trips most school holidays with lots of those being interstate. We went overseas also, NZ three times, toured a big part of USA for an 8-week family trip, went on a cruise to Noumea and Isle of Pines, and with the scouts I went to Japan for 4 weeks as a volunteer at a World Scout Jamboree.

While focusing on family life, I gave up hospitality to be a Teacher Aide and was also volunteering as a Cub Scout leader. Both allowed me to be around for the boys and not work nights, it also gave me opportunities for school and scout camps!

Then as if history was repeating itself, while living in Moranbah I separated from my then husband, my eldest graduated high school and moved to Melbourne to follow his dream, my youngest moved south with his father. And I went back to waitressing at that same motel in Moranbah, that I moved there for in the first place.

The Manager at the time of me working there originally and I were, and still are, great friends and it still had the same owner, so I got the job second time round a lot easier that the first time. I also stayed working in school, because I had landed a position as a Teacher Aide: Education Interpreter for Deaf and Hard of Hearing students, a job I was loving and I began studying Certificates in Auslan, for my new goal of Professional Auslan Interpreter.

Queensland- Back to Moranbah

There we have it, the first part, and if you missed what I was trying to show you, it is simply that I love to travel, I have travelled all my life and I have loved all of it. I am grateful of the life my parents gave me. I consider myself lucky to have experienced all of that. My only regret, not trying harder for the El Questro job.

Part 2 A.C.

After Covid-

I feel like the world got a little crazier after Covid19. I'm not sure why. I guess we all coped with lock downs in our own unique ways, and that's put us on different paths.

Me? Well this is where the duck story starts! But it's not just about ducks. It's about an idea. A dream that became as a result of the ducks! Confused? Let me catch you up, but we must go back just a little to the lock down part first. I know no-one wants to relive that. But I was in country Queensland, ours didn't last long, so hang in there.

Covid hits and living in a small country town had its benefits. We didn't have many full on lock downs as such. Not like what my son had in Melbourne, I think we were a month, if that,

Part 2 A.C.

tops! And working in education I was an "essential worker" so not much changed, until the school holidays, when for once I couldn't head off on a road trip or camping.

The local community radio station 4RFM decided to run a competition.

Simple enough; a challenge would be posted every day, you needed to complete the challenge and for evidence upload a photo or yourself doing it on the Facebook page.

My problem, I didn't want my face all over social media. My solution, a proxy!

Lucky9

I happened to have this little rubber duck that I had found the year earlier. His name was Lucky9 because after walking around in circles for hours at the local Relay For Life event, I spotted him in the grass. He had a 9 underneath him.

I contacted the radio station to see if I was still eligible for the competition and $500 prize money if I used Lucky9 as my substitute in photos. They said yes... I later realised I should have thought this through a bit more.

The challenges came posted every day. Most Lucky9 could do. The 80's work out was not one of them though! And the floor is lava was a certain challenge but we made it work. One task was to start an Instagram page for your pet.

At that time I had some guppies that spent their time having babies then eating them, and a rubber duck.

The duck won and the Instagram page was made. This was the turning point! Not for the competition. But for life.

Lucky 9

venturing.ducks

Liked by ███████ and **5 others**
venturing.ducks A bit of fishing...
4rfmcommunity Welcome to the hunt Ducky!!
3 May 2020

CatDuck

What I didn't realise then was that this was the start of another arrow to follow, another path to take. Funny thing was that year I was given an inspiration bangle for Christmas by a good friend. The words on it "She believed she could- and she did" I still wear this now and look to it for inspiration.

Over the next year I continued to study Auslan to work and to travel. But now when I traveled, I would upload the travels on Lucky9's Insta page.

After bit of a clean-up at the house I found I had a stack of rubber ducks. One little one was unique it was a duck with cat ears and whiskers. This one I had found in a Geocache in Utah, USA back in 2015. I decided that CatDuck was the perfect travel companion for Lucky9 and their adventures began.

CatDuck

venturing.ducks

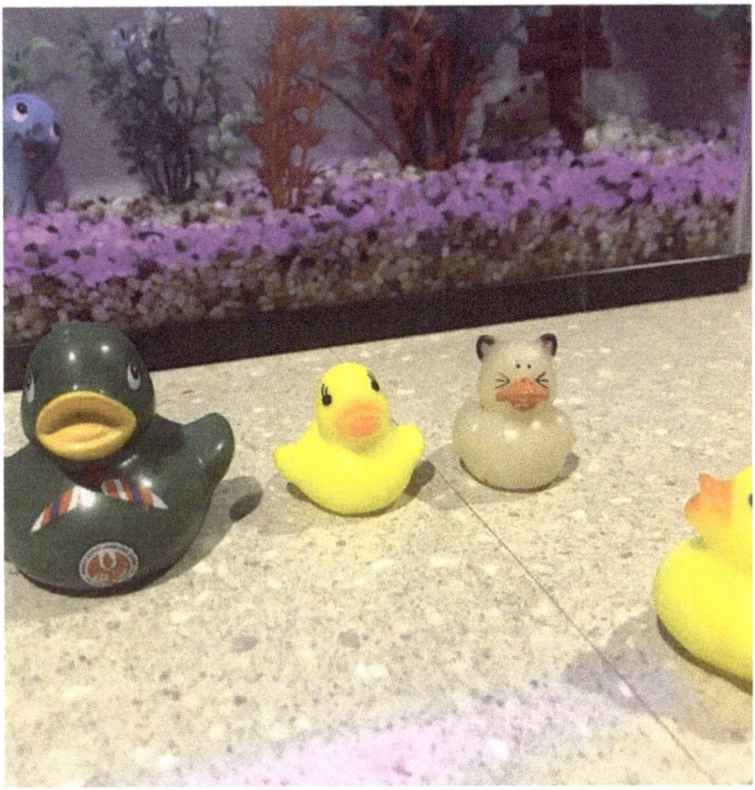

❤️ 💬 ➤ 🔖

 Liked by ████████ and **6 others**

venturing.ducks Lucky9 had a clean up today and found some old friends. Meet "WSJ duck" "Lucky17" and "cat-duck" lets see what adventures they get up to now!

16 May 2020

Mackay – Queensland

It was time for another move for me and I packed up and moved east to Mackay to persue my new plan.

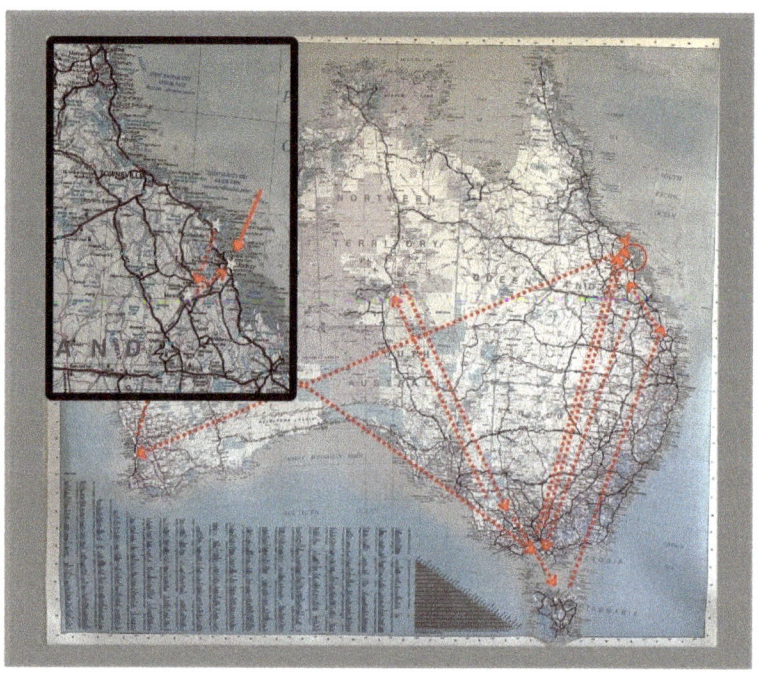

The book about a book.

VENTURING.DUCKS
Posts

venturing.ducks

   Liked by  and **7 others**

venturing.ducks New home for the ducks for a little while. Time to Begin Anew #zibutattoo

 She believed she could... so she did 💕

14 December 2020

Plans change

In Mackay I could be closer to the Deaf community and learn more so I could follow the Professional interpreting plan, the one where I would be able to eventually travel Australia and Interpret virtually on the road wherever I was.

As with all great plans, some just don't end up how you think they will. The more I studied and the more research I did I realised Professional was not the way I wanted to go. I believe with a lot of hard work and determination I would have achieved this. Because if I believe I can, I will!

But being in school, interpreting with the Deaf children was more my style. I was still picking up bar work at festivals, and able to travel in the school holidays, more camping, more road trips, more duck photos.

Plans change

venturing.ducks

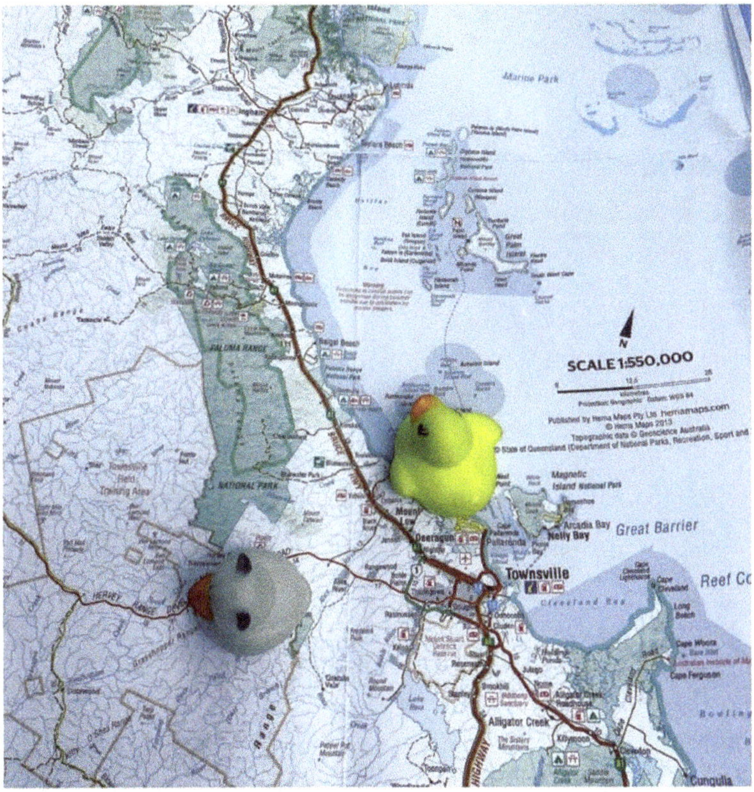

Liked by ███████████ and **6 others**
venturing.ducks Team meeting, CatDuck wants to go west and escape the traffic, Lucky9 wants to go north on the coast road.....

26 June 2021

The book about a book.

venturing.ducks

 Liked by ████████ and **7 others**
venturing.ducks Geocaching and creek camping. Loving the outdoors.

26 September 2021

Plans change

venturing.ducks

 Liked by ▓▓▓▓ and **7 others**
venturing.ducks Playing in the snow at Mount Wellington, got hit by a snowball!
24 September 2022

The new plan

My partner (who I met camping of course) and I have plans to travel, no surprise there, it's in my blood. But not just the travel during the holidays type of travel. We want the, sell everything and live on the road plan. The life I dreamed of as a little girl after moving so many places. No fixed address! This is my kind of perfect.

The problem. I am way off retirement age! So, the research began again. I want to do this, I want to follow this arrow, how do we make this work! Turns out there is an app for that! And there are sites and apps that help you find work on the road, I'm not afraid to get my hands dirty so that will work well. But still wanting to have some kind of steady income I started looking up "side hustles."

Have you searched this! Go check it out. There are so many!

Kindle Direct Publishing- KDP

After being part of pyramid schemes and other such selling programs, I was hesitant. Influencers pull some good pay, but that's just not my style.

Then I came across several publishing courses, claiming you could make the big dollars from a passive income, but you had to play the long game. I love books, I love creating, this looked like something that might suit me, so after a few webinars and lots of you tube watching i had a new direction.

I set up an Amazon and Kindle Direct Publishing account. Over 6 weeks I created 4 low content books. An RV journal and camping logbook, a notebook for the shed, a plain notebook, and a mixed pages journal for those who don't know what they want. The Pen Name for these books Venturing Ducks. I uploaded them one at a time as I finished them, my first one went live mid Nov, and I have sold 90 books in 10 weeks in 3 different countries. I'm still so shocked at this.

The book about a book.

VENTURING.DUCKS
Posts

● Liked by ▒▒▒▒▒
venturing.ducks Sold 50 books in 30 days 🥳, thanks for everyone's support #venturingducks

15 December 2023

Amazon

While looking into the books on Amazon I realised that there was this whole market out there for ecommerce within the Amazon FBA model. This would mean I could sell books and products through Amazon while on the road, no need for stock storage, no shop to look after. Just a laptop some internet and the road.

By now there are arrows everywhere and I want to follow them all, I can see so many opportunities. And I believe I will succeed!

Jumping in feet first as I do. I organise all things needed for a business and trademark the Venturing Ducks name, I build a website, sort out more social media platforms and feel like I have a plan in place!

The ducks will promote their travels on social media, the Amazon account will sell (once I purchase something) goods related to travel and/or camping in the Australian Amazon store. KDP will sell paperbacks and ebooks all over the world, with low content at the start but building up to travel guides of places we visit, and maybe children's travel books.

The VenturingDucks website will link it all together, Amazon, KDP, social media and travel blogs! Sounds legit to me! And I have had crazier ideas in my life!

Sometimes you just have to ignore the *what if I fail*, and focus on the *but what if i succeed!*

The book about a book

So how did we get to this book you are now reading! Well, this is a book I never intended to write until 5 days ago!

As we know algorithms rule the tech world. And up popped another add for a publishing course: but this one was about Audible. Not something I had thought about, I watched the webinar. Then read the "Bonus" book that came with it. Everything looked great, although my mind is still not made up on the use of Ghost writers and AI. I can see the benefit in both and apparently there are a lot more ghost written books than I realised, even ones I have read before.

Anyway, knowing that I'm in this for the long haul and not going to make hundreds overnight I did more research and found another roadblock. The company used to translate the transcript into the Audio books on Audible is not available for us Aussies yet. Bugger! Ok new plan, check out other audio book companies.

While starting that research, yes Google and I are close, I got an email from the company of that last webinar I did. They

The book about a book

were offering a "7 day Amazon Publishing Challenge." They take you from start to finish in writing and publishing a book and it will not cost a cent. Ok I'm in, what have I got to lose.

They didn't claim that your book would be a best seller, I think the reference was that your book may be like that first pancake in the batch that is never perfect, but they did offer step by step guidance. As you may have worked out. I'm up for a challenge. And I want to believe my book can be one of those pancakes mid batch!

So, this is *the book about a book* that may or may not make it. But it's going out there in the big wide world. It will be available in paperback, eBook and hopefully as an audiobook in lots of countries. If you are reading this now! Thank you! This is the proof that you only need to believe you can!

If no one reads it, I've lost nothing, because even the time taken to make this book has been an enjoyable leaning experience and as we all know, we learn best from our mistakes!

The End

That's it, we got to the end of the book. No ghost writer, no AI assistance, no Grammarly. Just raw words on a page and a little help with the formatting to fit it on the page to be published.

Now I have one favour to ask. If you are still reading, can you please jump back online and give a review or click on the stars for me. Yes, it helps with sales, but this review isn't for that purpose.

It's for all the people who don't have the belief in themselves that they can follow their dreams! That they can do something that they want to, that they don't have to give up. Let's show them all that all you have to do is believe in yourself.

An end note- for those who want to see if this book can actually sell. I'll have a sales counter up on the www.venturing-ducks.com website.

It will be in the bookshelf and is for this book alone. This book will be published at end of Jan 2024 so I'll update it at the end of every month and together we can see where it goes.

The End

If you would like to learn more about the Venturing Ducks and to see what the outcome of my little dream is check out the website and follow on whichever platform you prefer.

———————————————

www.ingramcontent.com/pod-product-compliance
Lightning Source LLC
Chambersburg PA
CBHW062105290426
44110CB00022B/2718